Tucholsky Wagner Zola Scott Sydow Freud Schlegel
Turgenev Wallace Fonatne Schlegel
Twain Walther von der Vogelweide Fouqué Friedrich II. von Preußen
Weber Freiligrath Frey
Fechner Fichte Weiße Rose von Fallersleben Kant Ernst Frommel
Richthofen
Engels Fielding Hölderlin
Fehrs Faber Flaubert Eichendorff Tacitus Dumas
Eliasberg Ebner Eschenbach
Feuerbach Maximilian I. von Habsburg Fock Eliot Zweig
Ewald Vergil
Goethe Elisabeth von Österreich London
Mendelssohn Balzac Shakespeare Dostojewski Ganghofer
Trackl Lichtenberg Rathenau Doyle Gjellerup
Mommsen Stevenson Tolstoi Hambruch
Thoma Lenz Hanrieder Droste-Hülshoff
Dach Verne von Arnim Hägele Hauff Humboldt
Karrillon Reuter Rousseau Hagen Hauptmann Gautier
Garschin Defoe Baudelaire
Damaschke Descartes Hebbel
Wolfram von Eschenbach Hegel Kussmaul Herder
Dickens Schopenhauer
Bronner Darwin Melville Grimm Jerome Rilke George
Campe Horváth Aristoteles Bebel Proust
Bismarck Vigny Barlach Voltaire Federer Herodot
Gengenbach Heine
Storm Casanova Tersteegen Gilm Grillparzer Georgy
Chamberlain Lessing Langbein Gryphius
Brentano Lafontaine
Strachwitz Claudius Schiller Kralik Iffland Sokrates
Katharina II. von Rußland Bellamy Schilling
Gerstäcker Raabe Gibbon Tschechow
Löns Hesse Hoffmann Gogol Wilde Vulpius
Luther Heym Hofmannsthal Gleim
Roth Klee Hölty Morgenstern Goedicke
Luxemburg Heyse Klopstock Kleist
Puschkin Homer
Machiavelli La Roche Horaz Mörike Musil
Navarra Aurel Musset Kierkegaard Kraft Kraus
Nestroy Marie de France Lamprecht Kind Kirchhoff Hugo Moltke
Laotse Ipsen Liebknecht
Nietzsche Nansen Ringelnatz
Marx Lassalle Gorki Klett Leibniz
von Ossietzky May vom Stein Lawrence Irving
Petalozzi Knigge
Platon Pückler Michelangelo Kock Kafka
Sachs Poe Liebermann
de Sade Praetorius Mistral Zetkin Korolenko

The publishing house tredition has created the series **TREDITION CLASSICS**. It contains classical literature works from over two thousand years. Most of these titles have been out of print and off the bookstore shelves for decades.

The book series is intended to preserve the cultural legacy and to promote the timeless works of classical literature. As a reader of a **TREDITION CLASSICS** book, the reader supports the mission to save many of the amazing works of world literature from oblivion.

The symbol of **TREDITION CLASSICS** is Johannes Gutenberg (1400 – 1468), the inventor of movable type printing.

With the series, tredition intends to make thousands of international literature classics available in printed format again – worldwide.

All books are available at book retailers worldwide in paperback and in hardcover. For more information please visit: www.tredition.com

tredition was established in 2006 by Sandra Latusseck and Soenke Schulz. Based in Hamburg, Germany, tredition offers publishing solutions to authors and publishing houses, combined with worldwide distribution of printed and digital book content. tredition is uniquely positioned to enable authors and publishing houses to create books on their own terms and without conventional manufacturing risks.

For more information please visit: www.tredition.com

Punctuation A Primer of Information about the Marks of Punctuation and their Use Both Grammatically and Typographically

Frederick W. (Frederick William) Hamilton

Imprint

This book is part of the TREDITION CLASSICS series.

Author: Frederick W. (Frederick William) Hamilton
Cover design: toepferschumann, Berlin (Germany)

Publisher: tredition GmbH, Hamburg (Germany)
ISBN: 978-3-8491-8423-0

www.tredition.com
www.tredition.de

PREFACE

This book, like the others in this Part, makes no pretense at originality. The author has studied and compared a considerable number of works by the best authorities on the subject and has endeavored to adapt the best of their contents to the use of printers' apprentices.Every author has his own set of rules. At first sight, each set appears inconsistent with those given by other writers. This inconsistency, however, is generally more apparent than real. It arises from differences in point of view, method of approach, and system of classification.

An attempt has been made to compile from these sources a set of rules which would bring before the pupil a correct and comprehensive view of the best current usage, well illustrated by examples and accompanied by practical typographical hints. The fact has been kept steadily in mind that this book is intended for a certain definite class of pupils and no pains have been spared to fit it to their needs.

Any treatise consisting, as this one necessarily does, mainly of rules is practically useful only as a basis for constant and persistent drill. It is, of course, valuable for reference, but the emergencies of the day's work leave no time for consultation. These rules must be learned, and not only learned but assimilated so that their correct application becomes instinctive and instantaneous. This result can be secured only by practice. Hence the emphasis laid on the exercises indicated in the paragraphs introductory to the review questions.

CONTENTS

INTRODUCTION

Punctuation is a device by which we aid words to tell their story. Words have done this at times without such aid, and may now do so, but at constant risk of serious misunderstanding. This can be easily seen by reading the following lines printed as they would have been written in an ancient manuscript.

WETHEPEOPLEOFTHEUNITEDSTATES
INORDERTOFORMAMOREPERFECT
UNIONESTABLISHJUSTICEINSUREDO
MESTICTRANQUILITYPROVIDEFOR
THECOMMONDEFENCEPROMOTETHE
GENERALWELFAREANDSECURETHE
BLESSINGSOFLIBERTYTOOURSELVES
ANDOURPOSTERITYDOORDAINAND
ESTABLISHTHISCONSTITUTIONFOR
THEUNITEDSTATESOFAMERICA

Probably this particular passage could be read without danger of serious misunderstanding. The two well-known passages which follow, however, are cases where either a simple statement may become a ridiculous travesty or a serious arraignment may become a eulogy by punctuation.

Punctuate the following so as to express two very different meanings:

Lord Palmerston then entered on his head a white hat upon his feet large but well polished boots upon his brow a dark cloud in his hand a faithful walking stick in his eye a menacing glare saying nothing.

[2]

Punctuate the following in two ways: one to represent a very bad man, and the other a very good man:

He is an old man and experienced in vice and wickedness he is never found in opposing the works of iniquity he takes delight in the downfall of his neighbors he never rejoices in the prosperity of his fellow-creatures he is always ready to assist in destroying the peace of society he takes no pleasure in serving the Lord he is uncommonly diligent in sowing discord among his friends and acquaintances he takes no pride in laboring to promote the cause of Christianity he has not been negligent in endeavoring to stigmatize all public teachers he makes no effort to subdue his evil passions he strives hard to build up satans kingdom he lends no aid to the support of the gospel among the heathen he contributes largely to the devil he will never go to heaven he must go where he will receive the just recompense of reward.

Punctuation being intended for the sole purpose of making the text intelligible and removing as many of the causes of possible misunderstanding as may be, must depend in the last resort on a correct understanding of the text. This understanding may be obtained from the text itself, from the context, that is, the writing as a whole, or from outside knowledge about the matter under consideration.

The prisoner said the witness was a sneak thief.

The prisoner, said the witness, was a sneak thief.

The meaning of this sentence depends entirely on the presence or absence of the two commas.

Manuscript comes in to the printer hastily written by the customer, author, or a reporter, or ticked over the telegraph wire, and there is little or no punctuation. Probably the context will supply the needed information and the line may be set up correctly. If there is no way of finding out [3] what the sentence means, follow copy. Insert no punctuation marks which you are not sure are needed.

Punctuation as we know it is of recent invention. The practice of the art of printing brought the necessity for a defined and systematized use of the points which had, most of them, long been in existence, but which had been used largely according to the personal preferences of the scribes or copyists. With the coming of the new methods of book reproduction came the recognized need for standardization and systematization.

The most ancient inscriptions and manuscripts are merely strings of letters, without spacing between words or sentences and without any points of any sort, like the example on page 1.

The first mark to be used was the dot, or period. Its original purpose was simply to furnish a resting place for the eye and the mind and so help a little in the grouping of the letters into words, clauses, and sentences, which the mind had hitherto been compelled to do unaided. It was used at the end of a sentence, at the end of a clause, to indicate abbreviations, to separate crowded words, especially where the sense was ambiguous (ANICEMAN might be either AN ICE MAN or A NICE MAN), or even as an æsthetic ornament between the letters of an inscription. In early manuscripts the period is usually placed high (˙) instead of low (.).

Sometimes a slanting mark (/) or a double dot (: or ..) was used to indicate the end of an important section of the writing or even of a sentence.

After a time spaces were introduced to show the grouping of the letters and the words. At first the sentences were separated by spaces, then the long words, and finally all words. In some languages, as in Italian, there are still combinations of long and short words, such as the combination of the pronoun with the verb, as in *datemi*, give me.

During the manuscript period different schools of copyists and even different individuals used different marks and different systems of pointing. For a considerable time the location of the dot indicated its force. Placed high (˙) it [4] had the force of a period. Placed in a middle position (·) it had the force of a comma. Placed low (.) it had the force of a semicolon. The rule, however, was not universally observed. A Latin manuscript of the seventh century has a high dot (˙) equivalent to a comma, a semicolon used as at present, and a dot accompanied by another dot or a dash to indicate the end of a sentence. A Latin manuscript of the ninth century shows the comma and an inverted semicolon ([;]) having a value between the semicolon and colon. Mediæval manuscript pointing, therefore, approximates modern forms in places, but lacks standardization into recognized systems.

The spread of printing brought new needs into prominence. The early printers used the period at the end of the sentence, the colon, and sometimes the slanting line (/). A reversed semicolon was used as a question mark. Wynkyn de Worde, Caxton's successor in the printing business in London, used five points in 1509. They were the period, the semicolon, the comma, the "interrogative," and the parenthesis.

The systematization of punctuation is due mainly to the careful and scholarly Aldus Manutius, who had opened a printing office in Venice in 1494. The great printers of the early day were great scholars as well. For a very long time the chief concern of the printer was the opening of the treasures of ancient thought to the world. They were therefore compelled to be the students, critics, and editors of the old manuscripts which served them as copy. They naturally took their punctuation from the Greek grammarians, but sometimes with changed meanings. The semicolon, for instance, is the Greek mark of interrogation.

The period took its name from the Greek word περίοδος, periodos, meaning a division of a sentence or a thought, as we to-day speak of an orator's eloquent periods.

The colon comes from the Greek κῶλον, kolon, meaning a limb.

The comma comes from the Greek κόμμα, komma, from κόπτειν, to cut.

The semicolon, of course, is the half colon. [5]

The question mark was made by writing the first and last letters of the Latin word *questio*, a question, vertically, ❡

The exclamation point was made by writing the letters of the Latin word *Io*, joy, vertically, ❡

The punctuation marks now in use and treated of in this book are as follows:

,   comma

;   semicolon

:   colon

.   period

?   interrogation

12

!	exclamation
( )	parentheses
[ ]	brackets
'	apostrophe
-	hyphen
—	dash
" "	quotation marks

Other important marks used by printers, but not, strictly speaking, marks of punctuation, are fully discussed in the volume on *Abbreviations and Signs* (No. 37) in this series.

There are two systems of punctuation in use, known respectively as the close and open systems. The close, or stiff, system, using points wherever they can be used, is of importance in precise composition of every sort, such as laws, contracts, legal and ecclesiastical statements, and the like. The open, or easy, system, omitting points wherever they can be omitted, is used generally in the commoner forms of composition. The tendency, sometimes pushed too far, is toward an extremely open style of punctuation. The general attitude of writers and printers may be summed up by saying that you must justify the use of a punctuation mark, particularly a comma, rather than its omission.

But why should the printer bother himself about punctuation at all? Is that not the business of the author, the editor, and the proofreader? Strictly speaking, yes, but authors generally neglect punctuation, copy is not usually carefully edited before going to the compositor, and proofreader's corrections are expensive. It is therefore important that the compositor should be intelligent about punctuation, whether he works in a large or a small office.

The question of how far the printer may go in changing or supplying the punctuation of copy will depend largely on [6] circumstances. If the condition of the manuscript is such as to show that the author really intended to put a fully punctuated, correctly spelled, and properly capitalized manuscript into the hands of the printer, he has a right to have his wishes respected even if his ideas are not those which prevail in the office. In such a case the compositor should follow copy literally. If any questions are to be raised they should be discussed by the proofreader *with the author*. The same rule holds in the case of manuscripts edited before being sent to the composing room. The editor has assumed all responsibility for the accuracy of the copy. In a great many cases the copy will come in carelessly written and wholly unedited. In such cases the compositor should punctuate as he goes along.

This is one of the tasks which subject the compositor to the test of intelligence. Printing is not now and never will be a purely mechanical trade. A printing office is no place for an apprentice who can not learn to think.

This book contains a description of the functions of the punctuation marks and the common rules for their use. Rules for the use of punctuation marks are very different from rules for the use of purely material things. They are useless unless applied intelligently. No set of rules could be devised which would work automatically or relieve the compositor from the necessity of thinking. Punctuation can never be reduced to an exact science.

Certain general directions should be borne in mind by writers and printers.

I. Learn by heart the rules for punctuation.

II. Note the peculiarities of the best writers and the best printers, especially in contemporary examples.

III. Pay constant attention to punctuation in everything you write.

IV. Punctuate your sentence while you are writing it.

V. Understand what you are printing. *This is of supreme importance.* Punctuation is an aid to understanding. You cannot correctly punctuate anything that you do not understand.

THE COMMA

The comma is by far the most difficult of all the punctuation marks to use correctly. Usage varies greatly from time to time and among equally good writers and printers at the same time. Certain general rules may be stated and should be learned. Many cases, however, will arise in which the rules will be differently interpreted and differently applied by different people.

The comma is the least degree of separation possible of indication in print. Its business is to define the particles and minor clauses of a sentence. A progressive tendency may be seen in the printing of English for centuries toward the elimination of commas, and the substitution of the comma for the semicolon and of the semicolon for the colon. Compare a page of the King James version of the Bible, especially in one of its earlier printings, with a page of serious discourse of to-day and the effects of the tendency will be easily seen. It is part of the general tendency toward greater simplicity of expression which has developed the clear and simple English of the best contemporary writers out of the involved and ornate style of the period of Queen Elizabeth. An ornate and involved style needs a good deal of punctuation to make it intelligible, while a simple and direct style needs but very little help.

This progressive change in the need for punctuation and in the attitude of writers toward it accounts for the difference in usage and for the difficulty in fixing rules to cover all cases. The present attitude toward punctuation, especially the use of the comma, is one of aversion. The writer is always held to justification of the presence of a comma rather than of its absence. Nevertheless it is quite possible to go too far in the omission of commas in ordinary writing. It is quite possible to construct sentences in such a way as to avoid their use. The result is a harsh and awkward style, unwarranted by any necessity. Ordinary [8] writing needs some use of commas to indicate the sense and to prevent ambiguity.

Always remember that the real business of the comma is just that of helping the meaning of the words and of preventing ambiguity by showing clearly the separation and connection of words and phrases. If there is possibility of misunderstanding without a comma, put one in. If the words tell their story beyond possibility of misunderstanding without a comma, there is no reason for its use. This rule will serve as a fairly dependable guide in the absence of any well recognized rule for a particular case, or where doubt exists as to the application of a rule.

Reversed, and usually in pairs, commas mark the beginning of a quotation.

In numerical statements the comma separates Arabic figures by triplets in classes of hundreds: $5,276,492.72.

In tabular work reversed commas are used as a sign for ditto.

SCHOOLS TEACHING PRINTING

Boston:	Boston Typothetæ School of Printing.
"	Industrial Arts High School.
Chicago:	Lakeside Press School of Printing.
"	Chicago Typothetæ School of Printing.
"	Lane Technical High School.

The comma is placed between the words which it is intended to separate. When used in connection with quotation marks, it is always placed inside them.

"Honesty is the best policy," as the proverb says.

Rules for the Use of the Comma

1. After each adjective or adverb in a series of two or more when not connected by conjunctions.

He was a tall, thin, dark man.

The rule holds when the last member of the series is preceded by a conjunction.

He was tall, thin, and dark.

[9]

The comma may be omitted when the words are combined into a single idea.

A still hot day.

An old black coat.

2. After each pair in a series of pairs of words or phrases not connected by conjunctions.

Sink or swim, live or die, survive or perish,

I give my hand and my heart to this vote.

Formerly the master printer, his journeymen,

even his apprentices, all lived in the same house.

3. To separate contrasted words.

We rule by love, not by force.

4. Between two independent clauses connected by a conjunction.

The press was out of order, but we managed to start it.

5. Before a conjunction when the word which preceded it is qualified by an expression which does not qualify the word which follows the conjunction.

He quickly looked up, and spoke.

6. Between relative clauses which explain the antecedent, or which introduce a new thought.

The type, which was badly worn, was not fit for the job.

If the relative clause limits the meaning of the antecedent, but does not explain it and does not add a new thought, the comma is not used.

He did only that which he was told to do.

7. To separate parenthetical or intermediate expressions from the context.

The school, you may be glad to know, is very successful.

[10]

The books, which I have read, are returned with gratitude.

He was pleased, I suppose, with his work.

If the connection of such expressions is so close as to form one connected idea the comma is not used.

The press nearest the south window is out of order.

If the connection of such expressions is remote, parentheses are used.

The Committee (appointed under vote of April 10, 1909) organized and proceeded with business.

8. To separate the co-ordinate clauses of compound sentences if such clauses are simple in construction and closely related.

He was kind, not indulgent, to his men; firm, but just, in discipline; courteous, but not familiar, to all.

9. To separate quotations, or similar brief expressions from the preceding part of the sentence.

Cæsar reported to the Senate, "I came, I saw, I conquered."

The question is, What shall we do next?

10. To indicate the omission of the verb in compound sentences having a common verb in several clauses.

One man glories in his strength, another in his wealth, another in his learning.

11. To separate phrases containing the case absolute from the rest of the sentence.

The form having been locked up, a proof was taken.

12. Between words or phrases in apposition to each other.

I refer to DeVinne, the great authority on Printing.

[11]

The comma is omitted when such an apposition is used as a single phrase or a compound name.

The poet Longfellow was born in Portland.

The word *patriotic* is now in extensive use.

13. After phrases and clauses which are placed at the beginning of a sentence by inversion.

Worn out by hard wear, the type at last became unfit for use.

Ever since, he has been fond of celery.

The comma is omitted if the phrase thus used is very short.

Of success there could be no doubt.

14. Introductory phrases beginning with *if, when, wherever, when-ever,* and the like should generally be separated from the rest of the sentence by a comma, even when the statement may appear to be direct.

When a plain query has not been answered, it is best to follow copy.

If the copy is hard to read, the compositor will set but few pages.

15. To separate introductory words and phrases and independent adverbs from the rest of the sentence.

Now, what are you going to do there?

I think, also, Franklin owed much of his success to his strong common sense.

This idea, however, had already been grasped by others.

Of course the comma is not used when these adverbs are used in the ordinary way.

They also serve who only stand and wait.

This must be done, however contrary to our inclinations.

[12]

16. To separate words or phrases of direct address from the context.

I submit, gentlemen, to your judgment.

From today, my son, your future is in your own hands.

17. Between the name of a person and his title or degree.

Woodrow Wilson, President of the United States.

Charles W. Eliot, LL.D.

18. Before the word *of* connecting a proper name with residence or position.

Senator Lodge, of Massachusetts.

Elihu B. Root, Senator from New York.

19. After the salutatory phrase at the beginning of a letter, when informal.

Dear John,

When the salutation is formal a colon should be used.

My dear Mr. Smith:

20. To separate the closing salutation of a formal letter from the rest of the sentence of which it forms a part.

Soliciting your continued patronage, I am,
Very sincerely yours,
John W. Smith.

21. To separate two numbers.

January 31, 1915.

By the end of 1914, 7062 had been built.

22. To indicate an ellipsis.

Subscription for the course, one dollar.

Exceptions to this rule are made in very brief sentences, especially in advertisements: Tickets 25 cents. Price one dollar.

[13] The foregoing rules for the use of the comma have been compiled from those given by a considerable number of authorities. Further examination of authorities would probably have added to the number and to the complexity of these rules. No two sets of rules which have come under the writer's observation are alike. Positive disagreements in modern treatises on the subject are few. The whole matter, however, turns so much on the use made of certain general principles and the field is so vast that different writers vary greatly in their statements and even in their ideas of what ought to be stated. It is very difficult to strike the right mean be-

tween a set of rules too fragmentary and too incomplete for any real guidance and a set of rules too long to be remembered and used.

After all possible has been done to indicate the best usage it remains true that the writer or the printer must, in the last resort, depend very largely on himself for the proper application of certain principles. The compositor may find himself helped, or restricted, by the established style of the office, or he may at times be held to strict following of copy. When left to himself he must be guided by the following general principles:

I. The comma is used to separate for the eye what is separate in thought.

The comma is not intended to break the matter up into lengths suited to the breath of one reading aloud.

The comma is not an æsthetic device to improve the appearance of the line.

II. The sole purpose of the comma is the unfolding of the sense of the words.

III. The comma cannot be correctly used without a thorough understanding of the sense of the words.

IV. In case of doubt, omit the comma.

[14]

THE SEMICOLON

The semicolon is used to denote a degree of separation greater than that indicated by the comma, but less than that indicated by the colon. It prevents the repetition of the comma and keeps apart the more important members of the sentence. The semicolon is generally used in long sentences, but may sometimes be properly used in short ones.

Rules for the Use of the Semicolon

1. When the members of a compound sentence are complex or contain commas.

Franklin, like many others, was a printer; but, unlike the others, he was student, statesman, and publicist as well.

With ten per cent of this flour the bread acquired a slight flavor of rye; fifteen per cent gave it a dark color; a further addition made the baked crumb very hard.

The meeting was composed of representatives from the following districts: Newton, 4 delegates, 2 substitutes; Dorchester, 6 delegates, 3 substitutes; Quincy, 8 delegates, 4 substitutes; Brookline, 10 delegates, 5 substitutes.

2. When the members of a compound sentence contain statements distinct, but not sufficiently distinct to be thrown into separate sentences.

Sit thou a patient looker-on;

Judge not the play before the play be done;

Her plot has many changes; every day

Speaks a new scene. The last act crowns the play.

3. When each of the members of a compound sentence makes a distinct statement and has some dependence [15] on statements in the other member or members of the sentence.

Wisdom hath builded her house; she hath hewn out her seven pillars; she hath killed her beasts; she hath mingled her wine; she hath furnished her table.

Each member of this sentence is nearly complete. It is not quite a full and definite statement, but it is much more than a mere amplification such as we might get by leaving out *she hath* every time after the first. In the former case we should use periods. In the latter we should use commas.

4. A comma is ordinarily used between the clauses of a compound sentence that are connected by a simple conjunction, but a semicolon may be used between clauses connected by conjunctive adverbs. Compare the following examples:

The play was neither edifying nor interesting to him, and he decided to change his plans.

The play was neither edifying nor interesting to him; therefore he decided to change his plans.

5. To indicate the chapter references in scriptural citations.

Matt. i: 5, 7, 9; v: 1-10; xiv: 3, 8, 27.

The semicolon should always be put outside quotation marks unless it forms a part of the quotation itself.

"Take care of the cents and the dollars will take care of themselves"; a very wise old saying.

[16]

THE COLON

The colon marks the place of transition in a long sentence consisting of many members and involving a logical turn of the thought. Both the colon and semicolon are much less used now than formerly. The present tendency is toward short, simple, clear sentences, with consequent little punctuation, and that of the open style. Such sentences need little or no aid to tell their story.

Rules for the Use of the Colon

1. Before *as, viz., that is, namely,* etc., when these words introduce a series of particular terms in apposition with a general term.

The American flag has three colors: namely, red, white, and blue.

2. Between two members of a sentence when one or both are made up of two or more clauses divided by semicolons.

The Englishman was calm and self-possessed; his antagonist impulsive and self-confident: the Englishman was the product of a volunteer army of professional soldiers; his antagonist was the product of a drafted army of unwilling conscripts.

3. Before particular elements in a definite statement.

Bad: He asked what caused the accident?
Right: He asked, "What caused the accident?"

Napoleon said to his army at the battle of the Pyramids: "Soldiers, forty centuries are looking down upon you."

The duties of the superintendent are grouped under three heads: first, etc.

[17] 4. Before formal quotations.

Write a short essay on the following topic: "What is wrong with our industrial system?"

When the formal introduction is brief, a comma may be used.

St. Paul said, "Bear ye one another's burdens."

5. After the formal salutatory phrase at the opening of a letter.

My dear Sir:

When the letter is informal use a comma.

Dear John,

6. Between the chapter and verse in scriptural references.

John xix: 22.

7. Between the city of publication and the name of the publisher in literary references.

"The Practice of Typography." New York: Oswald Publishing Company.

The colon has been similarly employed in the imprints on the title pages of books.

New York: Harper & Brothers, 1880.

DeVinne remarks upon this use of the colon that it is traditional and can not be explained.

The colon is sometimes used between the hours and minutes in indicating time, like: 11:42 a.m.

DeVinne does not approve of this, though other authorities give it as the rule. It is probably better to use the period in spite of its use as a decimal point, which use was probably the motive for seeking something else to use in writing time indications. In railroad printing the hour is often separated from the minutes by a simple space without any punctuation.

[18]

THE PERIOD

The period, or full stop, marks the end of a declarative sentence. As a sign it has several other uses which will appear in the paragraphs following.

Rules for the Use of the Period

1. At the end of every sentence unless interrogative or exclamatory.

2. After abbreviations.

Nicknames, *Sam*, *Tom*, etc., are not regarded as abbreviations.

The metric symbols are treated as abbreviations but the chemical symbols are not. M. (metre) and mg. (milligram) but H_2O and Na Cl.

Per cent is not regarded as an abbreviation.

The names of book sizes (12mo 16mo) are not regarded as abbreviations.

The period is now generally omitted in display matter after

Running heads,

Cut-in side-notes,

Central head-lines,

Box heads in tables,

Signatures at the end of letters.

The period is omitted

After Roman numerals, even though they have the value of ordinals.

After MS and similar symbols.

In technical matter, after the recognized abbreviations for linguistic epochs. IE (Indo-European), MHG (Middle High German)

[19] and after titles of well-known publications indicated by initials such as AAAPS (Annals of the American Academy of Political Science).

When a parenthesis forms the end of a declarative sentence the period is placed outside the parenthesis, as in the preceding example. A period is placed inside a parenthesis only in two cases.

1. After an abbreviation.

This was 50 years ago (i.e. 1860 A.D.)

2. At the end of an independent sentence lying entirely within the parenthesis.

Lincoln was at the height of his powers in 1860 (He was elected to the presidency at this time.)

When a sentence ends with a quotation, the period always goes inside the quotation marks.

I have just read DeVinne's "Practice of Typography."

The same rule applies to the use of the other low marks, comma, semicolon, and colon, in connection with quotation marks. Unlike most rules of grammar and punctuation, this rule does not rest on a logical basis. It rests on purely typographic considerations, as the arrangement of points indicated by the rule gives a better looking line than can be secured by any other arrangement.

Other Uses of the Period

1. The period is used as a decimal point.

2. The period is used in groups, separated by spaces, to indicate an ellipsis.

He read as follows: "The gentleman said . . . .

he was there and saw . . . . the act in question."

[20]

THE DASH

The dash is a very useful mark which has been greatly overworked by careless writers. It is very easy to make in manuscript and serves as a convenient cover for the writer's ignorance of what point should properly be used.

The conspicuousness of the dash makes it a very useful mark for guiding the eye of the reader to the unity of the sentence. It is particularly useful in legal pleadings where there is much repetition of statement and great elaboration of detail. In such cases commas, semicolons, and even parentheses are so multiplied that the relation of the clauses is lost sight of. The confusion thus arising may often be cleared up by intelligent use of the dash.

The dash is sometimes used to connect a side heading with the text that follows, or to connect the end of that text with the name of the writer.

A Rule for Peace. — If it be possible, as much as lieth in you, live peaceably with all men. — *St. Paul.*

The dash is sometimes used in catalogue work as a ditto mark.

De Vinne, Theodore Low. Historic Printing Types. New York, 1886.

— —The Invention of Printing. Francis Hart & Co., New York, 1878.

— —Plain Printing Types. Oswald Publishing Co., New York, 1914.

French printers use the dash in printing dialogue as a partial substitute for quotation marks. Quotation marks are placed at the beginning and end of the dialogue and a dash precedes each speech. This form is used even if the dialogue is extended over many pages.

[21]

Rules for the Use of the Dash

1. To mark abrupt changes in sentiment and in construction.

Have you ever heard — but how should you hear?

2. To mark pauses and repetitions used for dramatic or rhetorical effect.

They make a desert, and call it — peace.

Thou, great Anna, whom three states obey,

Who sometimes counsel takes — and sometimes tea.

3. To express in one sentence great contrariety of action or emotion or to increase the speed of the discourse by a succession of snappy phrases.

She starts — she moves — she seems to feel

The thrill of life along her keel.

In this connection DeVinne gives the following excellent example from Sterne:

Nature instantly ebbed again; — the film returned to its place; — the pulse fluttered, — stopped, — went on, — throbbed, — stopped again, — moved, — stopped, — Shall I go on? — No.

Attention may be called to Sterne's use of the semicolon and the comma with the dash, a use now obsolete except in rare cases.

4. To separate the repetition or different amplifications of the same statement.

The infinite importance of what he has to do — the goading conviction that it must be done — the dreadful combination in his mind of both the necessity and the incapacity — the despair of crowding the concerns of an age into a moment — the impossibility of beginning a repentance which should have been completed — of setting about a peace which should have been concluded — of suing for a pardon which should have been [22] obtained — all these complicated concerns intolerably augment the sufferings of the victims.

5. At the end of a series of phrases which depend upon a concluding clause.

Railroads and steamships, factories and warehouses, wealth and luxury — these are not civilization.

6. When a sentence is abruptly terminated.

If I thought he said it I would —

7. To precede expressions which are added to an apparently completed sentence, but which refer to some previous part of the sentence.

He wondered what the foreman would say — he had a way of saying the unexpected.

8. To connect extreme dates in time indication.

The war of 1861—1865. The war of 1861-1865.

9. To define verse references in the Bible or page references in books.

Matt. v: 1—11.Matt. v: 1-11.

See pp. 50—53.See pp. 50-53.

Note. In instances such as given in the two preceding rules the en dash may sometimes serve if the em dash appears too conspicuous.

10. A dash preceded by a colon is sometimes used before a long quotation forming a new paragraph. In other cases no point need accompany the dash.

The dash is sometimes used as a substitute for commas. Writers on the subject say that this use occurs when the connection between the parenthetical clause and the context is closer than would be indicated by commas. The distinction, if real, is difficult to see. It would be better if none but the most experienced writers attempted the use of the dash in this way.

Dashes are often used instead of marks of parenthesis. It is better to let each mark do its own work.

[23]

THE PARENTHESIS

The parenthesis, commonly used in pairs, encloses expressions which have no essential connection with the rest of the sentence, but are important to its full comprehension. It is liable to be neglected by writers because the dash is easier to make, and by printers because it is generally thought to mar the beauty of the line. Its distinct uses, however, should not be neglected.

Rules for the Use of the Parenthesis

1. To introduce into a sentence matter which is not essentially connected with the rest of the sentence, but aids in making it clear.

Trouble began when the apprentice (who had been strictly forbidden to do so) undertook to do some work on his own account.

This year (1914) saw the outbreak of a general war.

2. In reports of speeches to enclose the name of a person who has been referred to, or to indicate expressions on the part of the audience.

The honorable gentleman who has just spoken (Mr. Lodge) has no superior on this floor in his knowledge of international law. (Applause.)

3. Parentheses enclosing interrogation points or exclamation points are sometimes introduced into a sentence to cast doubt on a statement or to express surprise or contempt.

He said that on the fifth of January (?) he was in New York.

This most excellent (!) gentleman.

4. Parentheses are used, generally in pairs, sometimes singly, to enclose the reference letters or figures used to [24] mark division and classification in arguments or in precise statements.

This is done because: (a) it is clearer; (b) it is shorter.

These signs may be printed in several ways.

(a) a) (a) a) (1) 1) (1) 1)

The old-fashioned form of parenthesis, always made too thin, may need a thin space between it and its adjoining character when it is placed too close to any letter that nearly fills the body in height, as in (Hall). The space may not be needed when the proximate character has a shoulder, as in (Art), or when the parenthesis follows a period.)

The italic form of parenthesis is objectionable in book work. Distinction is sought for the word in italic and not for the parenthesis enclosing the word. The italic parenthesis may be used in job-work or full display lines of italic letters.

[25]

THE BRACKET

Brackets are used in pairs, like the parentheses. In Job composition either brackets or parentheses may be used, as suits the fancy or is convenient. In descriptive text matter, however, brackets should not be used where parentheses are clearly indicated.

Rules for the Use of the Bracket

1. To enclose words or phrases which are entirely independent of the rest of the sentence.

The enclosed words are usually comments, queries, corrections, criticisms, or directions inserted by some person other than the original writer or speaker.

2. To enclose passages of doubtful authenticity in reprints of early manuscripts, special amendments to bills under legislative consideration, or any other portions of a text which need peculiar identification.

3. In legal or ecclesiastical papers to indicate numerical words which may have to be changed, or to indicate where details are to be supplied.

This is the first [*second or third*] publication.

The officers shall remain in office [*here state the time*] or until their successors are duly qualified.

4. To avoid the confusion caused by a parenthesis within a parenthesis.

5. A single bracket is used to enclose the ending of a long line of poetry which will not fit the register and has to be run over into an adjoining line.

Doubt whether to use parentheses or brackets can usually be settled by this general principle:

Parentheses always enclose remarks apparently made by the writer of the text. Brackets enclose remarks certainly made by the editor or reporter of that text.

[26]

THE INTERROGATION

The interrogation is the point that asks questions. It should always be placed outside quotation marks unless it is a part of the quotation itself.

Rules for the Use of the Interrogation

1. The interrogation point is used at the end of every direct question.

Are you there?

Indirect questions, that is, statements that a question has been asked, do not require the interrogation.

He asked me if I was there.

He asked the question, Are you there? and received no answer.

2. At the end of each of a series of questions thrown into a single sentence.

Did he speak in an ordinary tone? or shout? or whisper?

3. The interrogation, like a certain inflection in the voice, may indicate that a sentence, though declarative in form, is really a question and requires an answer.

You are, of course, familiar with New York?

[27]

THE EXCLAMATION

The exclamation mark is the mark of strong emotion.

Rules for the Use of the Exclamation

1. After every expression of great surprise or emotion.

Look, my lord! it comes!

Angels and ministers of grace defend us!

Alas! my father.

2. After interjections and other exclamatory words.

Hurrah! Good! Away! Oh!

Where the exclamations are repeated without particularly emphasizing each one, each may be followed by a comma except the last.

Ha, ha, ha! That's a good joke!

O used as a vocative or to express a desire or imprecation does not call for an exclamation.

O John.

Oh, yes.

O, that night would come!

The exclamation is sometimes used in job printing to fill out a display line or for other inadequate reasons. These uses should be avoided.

[28]

THE APOSTROPHE

The apostrophe is primarily the sign of the possessive case, but it has several other uses.

Rules for the Use of the Apostrophe

1. The apostrophe for the possessive case is added only to nouns, not to the pronouns, which have their distinct possessive forms. *Its* is a possessive pronoun. *It's* is an abbreviation for *it is*. Do not use an apostrophe with the possessive adjectives *hers, ours, yours, theirs, its*.

2. All nouns in the singular and all nouns in the plural except those ending in *s* take an apostrophe and *s* to form the possessive.

Nouns in the plural ending in *s* take an apostrophe only to form the possessive.

There is much difference of opinion as to the invariability of the rule concerning singular nouns in *s*. DeVinne advises following the pronunciation. Where the second *s* is not pronounced, as often happens, to avoid the prolonged hissing sound of another *s*, he recommends omitting it in print.

Moses' hat, for Moses's hat.

For conscience' sake.

3. The apostrophe indicates the omission of letters in dialect, in familiar dialogue, and in poetry.

That's 'ow 'tis.

'Twas ever thus.

When two words are practically made into one syllable, a thin space may be put before the apostrophe, except that *don't*, *can't*, *won't*, and *shan't* are consolidated. This use of a space serves to distinguish between the possessive in *s* and the contraction of *is*.

Where death 's abroad and sorrow 's close behind.

[29] 4. Figures expressing dates are often abbreviated, but it is not good general practice.

The boys of '61.

It happened in '14.

5. The apostrophe is used to form the plural of letters and figures.

Cross your t's and dot your i's.

Make 3's and 5's more plain.

Except in these cases the apostrophe is not a plural sign and should be so used only when it is intended to reproduce a dialect or colloquialism.

Wrong: All the Collins's were there.

Right: All the Collinses were there.

The final *ed* of past tenses and past participles was formerly pronounced as a distinct syllable, thus: *clos-ed*, *belov-ed*, and this pronunciation continued in common use in poetry long after it was discontinued in prose. During this period of transition the modern pronunciation was indicated by dropping the *e* and using an apostrophe, thus: *clos'd*, *belov'd*. It is now understood that while the full spelling is to be used, the old pronunciation is not to be used unless specially indicated by placing a grave accent over the *e* of the last syllable, thus: *belovèd*.

At the same period poets, especially, used an apostrophe to indicate a silent *e* as in *ev'ry*, but the usage is now obsolete.

Such abbreviations as *Dep't, Gov't, Sec'y*, and the like, are objectionable in print. If such abbreviations are necessary it is better to use the forms *Dept., Govt., Secy.*

[30]

THE HYPHEN

The hyphen is used to join compound words; to mark the division of a word too long to go entirely into one line; to separate the syllables of words in order to show pronunciation; as a leader in tabular work. For this last purpose the period is to be preferred to any other mark in use. Tabular work without leaders is obscure and therefore objectionable.

[31]

QUOTATION MARKS

Quotation marks are signs used to indicate that the writer is giving exactly the words of another. A French printer named Morel used a comma in the outer margin to indicate a quoted line about 1550. About a century later another Frenchman, Ménage, introduced a mark («») resembling a double parenthesis but shorter. These marks were cast on the middle of the type body so that they could be reversed for use at either the beginning or the end of a quotation. The French have retained these signs as their quotation marks ever since.

When the English adopted the use of quotation marks, they did not take over the French marks, but substituted two inverted commas at the beginning and two apostrophes at the end of the quoted paragraph. These marks are typographically unsatisfactory. They are weak and therefore hardly adequate to their purpose in aiding the understanding through the eye. Being cast on the upper part of the type body, they leave a blank space below and thus impair the beauty of the line and interfere with good spacing. Certain rules for the position of quotation marks when used with other marks are based upon these typographical considerations rather than upon logical considerations.

Rules for the Use of Quotation Marks

1. Every direct quotation should be enclosed in double quotation marks.

"I will go," said he, "if I can."

Reports of what another person has said when given in words other than his own are called indirect quotations and take no marks.

He said he would go if he could.

2. A quotation of several paragraphs requires quotation marks at the beginning of each paragraph, but at the end [32] of the last one only. In legal documents, and sometimes elsewhere, quotations are defined and emphasized by putting double commas at the beginning of every line of the quotation.

The same result may be better obtained by using smaller type, or indenting the quotation, or both.

3. A quotation included within another quotation should be enclosed by single quotation marks.

He said: "I heard him cry 'Put down that gun,' and then I heard a shot."

4. Titles of books, essays, art works, etc., are usually enclosed in quotation marks. When the books are supposedly familiar to all readers, the marks are not used. You would not print "The Bible," "Paradise Lost," "The Iliad."

The titles of books, etc., are sometimes printed in italics instead of being enclosed in quotation marks. This is a matter of office style rather than of good or bad practice.

5. In writing about plays or books, the name of the work may be quoted and the name of a character italicized. This is done to avoid confusion between the play, the character, and the real person portrayed. "William Tell" is a play. *William Tell* is a character in fiction. William Tell is a national hero of Switzerland.

This usage is by no means uniform; here again, we are on the ground of office style.

6. Names of vessels are sometimes quoted, sometimes italicized, and sometimes printed without distinguishing marks. Here we are once more on the ground of office style.

7. Sentences from a foreign language are usually enclosed in quotation marks. Single words or phrases are usually printed in italics. Both italics and quotation marks should not be used except under certain unusual conditions or when positively ordered by the author.

8. Quotation marks may be used with a word to which [33] the writer desires to attract particular attention or to which he desires to give an unusual, technical, or ironical meaning.

This "gentleman" needs a shave.

9. When a quotation is long or when it is introduced in a formal manner, it is usually preceded by a colon. Isolated words or phrases call for no point after the introductory clause. This is true when the phrases so quoted run to considerable length, provided there is no break in the flow of thought and expression.

10. When a quotation ends a sentence the quotation marks are placed after the period.

The comma is always placed inside the quotation marks.

The position of the other marks (semicolon, colon, exclamation, and interrogation) is determined by the sense. If they form a part of the matter quoted, they go inside the quote marks; if not, they go outside them.

11. When quotation marks occur at the beginning of a line of poetry, they should go back into the indention space.

"Breathes there a man with soul so dead
 Who never to himself hath said,
'This is my own, my native land'?"

This illustration is also a good example of the use of marks in combinations. We have first the single quotation marking the end of the included quotation, then the interrogation which ends the sentence, then the double quotation marks in their proper position.

Quotation marks should not be used needlessly. Very familiar expressions from the best known authors, such as *to the manor born, a conscience void of offence, with malice toward none and charity for all,* have become part of the current coin of speech and need not be quoted. Lists of words considered as words merely, lists of books or plays, and other such copy should be printed without quotation marks. Sprinkling a page thickly with quotation marks not only spoils its appearance but makes it hard to read, without adding to its clearness of meaning.

[34]

GENERAL REMARKS

Book titles are now set without points. This fashion was introduced by Pickering of London about 1850. This method is generally to the advantage of the title page thus treated. It is possible, however, to carry it too far and so to obscure the sense. Commas should not be omitted from firm names, such as Longmans, Green & Co., as in case of such omission there is no way of knowing whether one or more persons are indicated. Punctuation should not be omitted from the titles which may accompany an author's name, nor from the date if day and month are given as well as year.

Avoid the doubling of points wherever possible. When an abbreviation precedes a colon, omit the period. When an abbreviation precedes a comma, the period is often inserted, but in many cases one or the other can be dropped to advantage. The dash is not generally preceded by a comma, semicolon, or colon in current printing usage. A comma should rarely go before the first parenthesis. If used at all with the parentheses, it should follow the closing parenthesis. When a complete sentence is enclosed in parentheses, the period falls within the parentheses. When the enclosure is a brief passage at the end of a sentence, the period falls outside the parentheses.

Do not put a period before the apostrophe and the possessive *s* as in *Co.'s.* The word *Company* may be abbreviated to *Co.* although it is

not desirable to do so if it can be avoided. The possessive of *Co.* is
Co's.

[35]

SUMMARY

1. A comma separates clauses, phrases, and particles.

2. A semicolon separates different statements.

3. A colon is the transition point of the sentence.

4. A period marks the end of a sentence.

5. A dash marks abruptness or irregularity.

6. Parentheses enclose interpolations in the sentence.

7. Brackets enclose irregularities in the sentence.

8. An interrogation asks a question for an answer.

9. An exclamation marks surprise.

10. An apostrophe marks elisions and the possessive case.

11. Quotation marks define quoted words.

[36]

SUPPLEMENTARY READING

Correct Composition. By DeVinne. Oswald Publishing Company, New York.

The Writer's Desk Book. By William Dana Orcutt. Frederick A. Stokes Company, New York.

A Manual for Writers. By Manly and Powell. The University of Chicago Press, Chicago.

Composition and Rhetoric. By Lockwood and Emerson. Ginn & Co., Boston.

The Art of Writing and Speaking the English Language. By Sherwin Cody. The Old Greek Press, Chicago.

Handbook of Composition. By Edwin D. Woolley. D. C. Heath & Co., Boston.

English Composition, Book One, Enlarged. By Stratton D. Brooks. Ginn & Co., Boston.

[37]

REVIEW QUESTIONS

SUGGESTIONS TO STUDENTS AND INSTRUCTORS

The following questions, based on the contents of this pamphlet, are intended to serve (1) as a guide to the study of the text, (2) as an aid to the student in putting the information contained into definite statements without actually memorizing the text, (3) as a means of securing from the student a reproduction of the information in his own words.

A careful following of the questions by the reader will insure full acquaintance with every part of the text, avoiding the accidental omission of what might be of value. These primers are so condensed that nothing should be omitted.

In teaching from these books it is very important that these questions and such others as may occur to the teacher should be made the basis of frequent written work, and of final examinations.

The importance of written work cannot be overstated. It not only assures knowledge of material, but the power to express that knowledge correctly and in good form.

If this written work can be submitted to the teacher in printed form it will be doubly useful.

QUESTIONS

1. What is punctuation?

2. How were ancient manuscripts written?

3. What were the first punctuation marks, and how were they used?

4. What can you tell about punctuation marks in the manuscript period?

5. What can you tell about the punctuation of the early printers?

6. Who may be said to have systematized punctuation?

7. Give the names of the principal punctuation marks and the meaning of the names.

8. Give a list of the punctuation marks now in use and show how they are made.

9. Name and describe the two systems of punctuation.

10. What is the tendency in the use of punctuation?

11. Why is it necessary for a compositor to understand punctuation?

12. When should the compositor follow copy and when not?

13. What five general directions should always be remembered?

14. What is the comma used for?

[38] 15. What is the tendency in the use of commas?

16. What are reversed commas used for?

17. How are commas used with numerals?

18. How are commas used in table work?

19. How are commas placed in relation to the words whose meaning they help?

20. Give the rules for the use of the comma.

21. What are the four general principles for the use of the comma?

22. What is the semicolon used for?

23. Give the rules for the use of the semicolon.

24. What is the colon used for?

25. Give the rules for the use of the colon.

26. What is the period used for?

27. Where are periods used?

28. Where are periods omitted?

29. How do we use the period in connection with parentheses?

30. How do we use the period in connection with quotation marks?

31. What is the reason for this rule?

32. What other uses has the period?

33. What is the dash used for?

34. What special use of the dash is found in French books?

35. Give the rules for the use of the dash.

36. Are other punctuation marks used with the dash?

37. What is the parenthesis used for?

38. Give the rules for the use of the parenthesis.

39. When would you use letter spacing with the parenthesis, and why?

40. What use is made of the italic parenthesis?

41. Give the rules for the use of the brackets.

42. What is the distinction in use between the bracket and the parenthesis?

43. What is the interrogation point used for?

44. Give the rules for the use of the interrogation.

45. What is the exclamation point used for?

46. Give the rules for the use of the exclamation.

47. What is the apostrophe used for?

[39] 48. Give the rules for the use of the apostrophe.

49. What is the use of the apostrophe in past participles?

50. What is said of the use of the apostrophe in such abbreviations as *Dep't?*

51. What is the hyphen used for?

52. What are quotation marks used for?

53. Give the rules for the use of quotation marks.

54. When are quotation marks omitted?

55. How are book titles now punctuated?

56. Should punctuation marks be doubled?

57. How is the comma used with parentheses?

58. How would you punctuate the possessive of an abbreviation, for example, *the Doctor's house,* using the abbreviation *Dr.?*

59. Give a brief summarized statement of the use of the twelve punctuation marks.

[40]

GLOSSARY

Absolute — Free from the usual grammatical relations.

Antecedent — That to which a relative pronoun or a relative clause refers.

Apposition — When the meaning of a noun or pronoun is made clear or emphatic by the use of another noun or pronoun, the two are said to be in apposition.

Clause — A group of words consisting of a subject and predicate with their modifiers and forming a part of a sentence; a sentence within a sentence.

Compound Sentence — A sentence consisting of several clauses.

Coördinate Clauses — Clauses of equal rank.

Declarative Sentence — A sentence which states a fact.

Exclamatory Sentence—A sentence which utters an exclamation.

Independent Adverbs—Adverbs not in grammatical relations with other words in the sentence.

Interrogative Sentence—A sentence which asks a question.

Minor Clauses—Clauses other than the principal clause or main statement of a sentence.

Parenthetical—Incidental; not an essential part of a sentence or statement.

Particle—One of the minor parts of speech not inflected, that is, not undergoing changes in form.

Phrase—An expression consisting usually of but a few words, denoting a single idea, or forming a separate part of a sentence.

Relative Clause—A clause joined to the rest of the sentence by a relative pronoun.

Salutation—A form of greeting, especially at the beginning or end of a letter.

Salutatory Phrase—The words forming a salutation, or greeting.

[i]

TYPOGRAPHIC TECHNICAL SERIES FOR APPRENTICES

The following list of publications, comprising the Typographic Technical Series for Apprentices, has been prepared under the supervision of the Committee on Education of the United Typothetae of America for use in trade classes, in course of printing instruction, and by individuals.

Each publication has been compiled by a competent author or group of authors, and carefully edited, the purpose being to provide the printers of the United States—employers, journeymen, and apprentices—with a comprehensive series of handy and inexpensive compendiums of reliable, up-to-date information upon the various branches and specialties of the printing craft, all arranged in orderly fashion for progressive study.

The publications of the series are of uniform size, 5×8 inches. Their general make-up, in typography, illustrations, etc., has been, as far as practicable, kept in harmony throughout. A brief synopsis of the particular contents and other chief features of each volume will be found under each title in the following list.

Each topic is treated in a concise manner, the aim being to embody in each publication as completely as possible all the rudimentary information and essential facts necessary to an understanding of the subject. Care has been taken to make all statements accurate and clear, with the purpose of bringing essential information within the understanding of beginners in the different fields of study. Wherever practicable, simple and well-defined drawings and illustrations have been used to assist in giving additional clearness to the text.

In order that the pamphlets may be of the greatest possible help for use in trade-school classes and for self-instruction, each title is accompanied by a list of Review Questions covering essential items of the subject matter. A short Glossary of technical terms belonging to the subject or department treated is also added to many of the books.

These are the Official Text-books of the United Typothetae of America.

Address all orders and inquiries to Committee on Education, United Typothetae of America, Chicago, Illinois, U. S. A.

[ii]

PART I—*Types, Tools, Machines, and Materials*

• 1. Type: a Primer of Information By A. A. Stewart

Relating to the mechanical features of printing types; their sizes, font schemes, etc., with a brief description of their manufacture. 44 pp.; illustrated; 74 review questions; glossary.

• 2. Compositors' Tools and Materials By A. A. Stewart

A primer of information about composing sticks, galleys, leads, brass rules, cutting and mitering machines, etc. 47 pp.; illustrated; 50 review questions; glossary.

• 3. Type Cases, Composing Room Furniture By A. A. Stewart

A primer of information about type cases, work stands, cabinets, case racks, galley racks, standing galleys, etc. 43 pp.; illustrated; 33 review questions; glossary.

• 4. Imposing Tables and Lock-up Appliances By A. A. Stewart

Describing the tools and materials used in locking up forms for the press, including some modern utilities for special purposes. 59 pp.; illustrated; 70 review questions; glossary.

• 5. Proof Presses By A. A. Stewart

A primer of information about the customary methods and machines for taking printers' proofs. 40 pp.; illustrated; 41 review questions; glossary.

• 6. Platen Printing Presses By Daniel Baker

A primer of information regarding the history and mechanical construction of platen printing presses, from the original hand press to the modern job press, to which is added a chapter on automatic presses of small size. 51 pp.; illustrated; 49 review questions; glossary.

• 7. Cylinder Printing Presses By Herbert L. Baker

Being a study of the mechanism and operation of the principal types of cylinder printing machines. 64 pp.; illustrated; 47 review questions; glossary.

• 8. Mechanical Feeders and Folders By William E. Spurrier

The history and operation of modern feeding and folding machines; with hints on their care and adjustments. Illustrated; review questions; glossary.

• 9. Power for Machinery in Printing Houses By Carl F. Scott

A treatise on the methods of applying power to printing presses and allied machinery with particular reference to electric drive. 53 pp.; illustrated; 69 review questions; glossary.

• 10. Paper Cutting Machines By Niel Gray, Jr.

A primer of information about paper and card trimmers, hand-lever cutters, power cutters, and other automatic machines for cutting paper, 70 pp.; illustrated; 115 review questions; glossary.

• 11. Printers' Rollers By A. A. Stewart

A primer of information about the composition, manufacture, and care of inking rollers. 46 pp.; illustrated; 61 review questions; glossary.

• 12. Printing Inks By Philip Ruxton

Their composition, properties and manufacture (reprinted by permission from Circular No. 53, United States Bureau of Standards); together with some helpful suggestions about the everyday use of printing inks by Philip Ruxton. 80 pp.; 100 review questions; glossary.

[iii]

• 13. How Paper is Made By William Bond Wheelwright

A primer of information about the materials and processes of manufacturing paper for printing and writing. 68 pp.; illustrated; 62 review questions; glossary.

• 14. Relief Engravings By Joseph P. Donovan

Brief history and non-technical description of modern methods of engraving; woodcut, zinc plate, halftone; kind of copy for reproduction; things to remember when ordering engravings. Illustrated; review questions; glossary.

• 15. Electrotyping and Sterotyping By Harris B. Hatch and A. A. Stewart

A primer of information about the processes of electrotyping and stereotyping. 94 pp.; illustrated; 129 review questions; glossaries.

PART II — *Hand and Machine Composition*

• 16. Typesetting By A. A. Stewart

A handbook for beginners, giving information about justifying, spacing, correcting, and other matters relating to typesetting. Illustrated; review questions; glossary.

• 17. Printers' Proofs By A. A. Stewart

The methods by which they are made, marked, and corrected, with observations on proofreading. Illustrated; review questions; glossary.

• 18. First Steps in Job Composition By Camille DeVéze

Suggestions for the apprentice compositor in setting his first jobs, especially about the important little things which go to make good display in typography. 63 pp.; examples; 55 review questions; glossary.

• 19. General Job Composition

How the job compositor handles business stationery, programs and miscellaneous work. Illustrated; review questions; glossary.

• 20. Book Composition By J. W. Bothwell

Chapters from DeVinne's "Modern Methods of Book Composition," revised and arranged for this series of textbooks by J. W. Bothwell of The DeVinne Press, New York.

Part I: Composition of pages. Part II: Imposition of pages. 229 pp.; illustrated; 525 review questions; glossary.

- **21. Tabular Composition By Robert Seaver**

A study of the elementary forms of table composition, with examples of more difficult composition. 36 pp.; examples; 45 review questions.

- **22. Applied Arithmetic By E. E. Sheldon**

Elementary arithmetic applied to problems of the printing trade, calculation of materials, paper weights and sizes, with standard tables and rules for computation, each subject amplified with examples and exercises. 159 pp.

- **23. Typecasting and Composing Machines A. W. Finlay, Editor**

Section I — The Linotype **By L. A. Hornstein**
Section II — The Monotype **By Joseph Hays**
Section III — The Intertype **By Henry W. Cozzens**
Section IV — Other Typecasting and Typesetting Machines **By Frank H. Smith**

A brief history of typesetting machines, with descriptions of their mechanical principles and operations. Illustrated; review questions; glossary.

PART III — *Imposition and Stonework* [iv]

- **24. Locking Forms for the Job Press By Frank S. Henry**

Things the apprentice should know about locking up small forms, and about general work on the stone. Illustrated; review questions; glossary.

- **25. Preparing Forms for the Cylinder Press By Frank S. Henry**

Pamphlet and catalog imposition; margins; fold marks, etc. Methods of handling type forms and electrotype forms. Illustrated; review questions; glossary.

- **31. Book Binding By John J. Pleger**

Practical information about the usual operations in binding books; folding; gathering, collating, sewing, forwarding, finishing. Case making and cased-in books. Hand work and machine work. Job and blank-book binding. Illustrated; review questions; glossary.

PART VI — *Correct Literary Composition*

- **32. Word Study and English Grammar By F. W. Hamilton**

A primer of information about words, their relations, and their uses. 68 pp.; 84 review questions; glossary.

- **33. Punctuation By F. W. Hamilton**

A primer of information about the marks of punctuation and their use, both grammatically and typographically. 56 pp.; 59 review questions; glossary.

[v]

- **34. Capitals By F. W. Hamilton**

A primer of information about capitalization, with some practical typographic hints as to the use of capitals. 48 pp.; 92 review questions; glossary.

- **35. Division of Words By F. W. Hamilton**

Rules for the division of words at the ends of lines, with remarks on spelling, syllabication and pronunciation. 42 pp.; 70 review questions.

- **36. Compound Words By F. W. Hamilton**

A study of the principles of compounding, the components of compounds, and the use of the hyphen. 34 pp.; 62 review questions.

- **37. Abbreviations and Signs By F. W. Hamilton**

A primer of information about abbreviations and signs, with classified lists of those in most common use. 58 pp.; 32 review questions.

- **38. The Uses of Italic By F. W. Hamilton**

A primer of information about the history and uses of italic letters. 31 pp.; 37 review questions.

- **39. Proofreading By Arnold Levitas**

The technical phases of the proofreader's work; reading, marking, revising, etc.; methods of handling proofs and copy. Illustrated by examples. 59 pp.; 69 review questions; glossary.

- **40. Preparation of Printers' Copy By F. W. Hamilton**

Suggestions for authors, editors, and all who are engaged in preparing copy for the composing room. 36 pp.; 67 review questions.

- **41. Printers' Manual of Style**

A reference compilation of approved rules, usages, and suggestions relating to uniformity in punctuation, capitalization, abbreviations, numerals, and kindred features of composition.

- **42. The Printer's Dictionary By A. A. Stewart**

A handbook of definitions and miscellaneous information about various processes of printing, alphabetically arranged. Technical terms explained. Illustrated.

PART VII — *Design, Color, and Lettering*

- **43. Applied Design for Printers By Harry L. Gage**

A handbook of the principles of arrangement, with brief comment on the periods of design which have most influenced printing. Treats of harmony, balance, proportion, and rhythm; motion; symmetry and variety; ornament, esthetic and symbolic. 37 illustrations; 46 review questions; glossary; bibliography.

• 44. Elements of Typographic Design By Harry L. Gage

Applications of the principles of decorative design. Building material of typography paper, types, ink, decorations and illustrations. Handling of shapes. Design of complete book, treating each part. Design of commercial forms and single units. Illustrations; review questions; glossary; bibliography.

[vi]

• 45. Rudiments of Color in Printing By Harry L. Gage

Use of color: for decoration of black and white, for broad poster effect, in combinations of two, three, or more printings with process engravings. Scientific nature of color, physical and chemical. Terms in which color may be discussed: hue, value, intensity. Diagrams in color, scales and combinations. Color theory of process engraving. Experiments with color. Illustrations in full color, and on various papers. Review questions; glossary; bibliography.

• 46. Lettering in Typography By Harry L. Gage

Printer's use of lettering: adaptability and decorative effect. Development of historic writing and lettering and its influence on type design. Classification of general forms in lettering. Application of design to lettering. Drawing for reproduction. Fully illustrated; review questions; glossary; bibliography.

• 47. Typographic Design in Advertising By Harry L. Gage

The printer's function in advertising. Precepts upon which advertising is based. Printer's analysis of his copy.

Emphasis, legibility, attention, color. Method of studying advertising typography. Illustrations; review questions; glossary; bibliography.

• 48. Making Dummies and Layouts By Harry L. Gage

A layout: the architectural plan. A dummy: the imitation of a proposed final effect. Use of dummy in sales work. Use of layout. Function of layout man. Binding schemes for dummies. Dummy envelopes. Illustrations; review questions; glossary; bibliography.

PART VIII — *History of Printing*

• 49. Books Before Typography By F. W. Hamilton

A primer of information about the invention of the alphabet and the history of bookmaking up to the invention of movable types. 62 pp.; illustrated; 64 review questions.

• 50. The Invention of Typography By F. W. Hamilton

A brief sketch of the invention of printing and how it came about. 64 pp.; 62 review questions.

• 51. History of Printing — Part I By F. W. Hamilton

A primer of information about the beginnings of printing, the development of the book, the development of printers' materials, and the work of the great pioneers. 63 pp.; 55 review questions.

• 52. History of Printing — Part II By F. W. Hamilton

A brief sketch of the economic conditions of the printing industry from 1450 to 1789, including government regulations, censorship, internal conditions and industrial relations. 94 pp.; 128 review questions.

The estimator and his work; forms to use; general rules for estimating. Review questions. Glossary.

• 60. Estimating and Selling By Henry P. Porter

An insight into the methods used in making estimates, and their relation to selling. Review questions. Glossary.

• 61. Accounting for Printers By Henry P. Porter

A brief outline of an accounting system for printers; necessary books and accessory records. Review questions. Glossary.

PART X — *Miscellaneous*

• 62. Health, Sanitation, and Safety By Henry P. Porter

Hygiene in the printing trade; a study of conditions old and new; practical suggestions for improvement; protective appliances and rules for safety.

• 63. Topical Index By F. W. Hamilton

A book of reference covering the topics treated in the Typographic Technical Series, alphabetically arranged.

• 64. Courses of Study By F. W. Hamilton

A guidebook for teachers, with outlines and suggestions for classroom and shop work.

[viii]

ACKNOWLEDGMENT

This series of Typographic Text-books is the result of the splendid co-operation of a large number of firms and individuals engaged in the printing business and its allied industries in the United States of America.

The Committee on Education of the United Typothetae of America, under whose auspices the books have been prepared and published, acknowledges its indebtedness for the generous assistance rendered by the many authors, printers, and others identified with this work.

While due acknowledgment is made on the title and copyright pages of those contributing to each book, the Committee nevertheless felt that a group list of co-operating firms would be of interest.

The following list is not complete, as it includes only those who have co-operated in the production of a portion of the volumes, constituting the first printing. As soon as the entire list of books comprising the Typographic Technical Series has been completed (which the Committee hopes will be at an early date), the full list will be printed in each volume.

The Committee also desires to acknowledge its indebtedness to the many subscribers to this Series who have patiently awaited its publication.

Committee on Education,
United Typothetae of America.
Henry P. Porter, *Chairman,*
E. Lawrence Fell,
A. M. Glossbrenner,
J. Clyde Oswald,
Toby Rubovits.

Frederick W. Hamilton, *Education Director.*

[ix]

CONTRIBUTORS

For Composition and Electrotypes

Isaac H. Blanchard Company, New York, N. Y.
S. H. Burbank & Co., Philadelphia, Pa.
J. S. Cushing & Co., Norwood, Mass.
The DeVinne Press, New York, N. Y.
R. R. Donnelley & Sons Co., Chicago, Ill.
Geo. H. Ellis Co., Boston, Mass.
Evans-Winter-Hebb, Detroit, Mich.
Franklin Printing Company, Philadelphia, Pa.
F. H. Gilson Company, Boston, Mass.
Stephen Greene & Co., Philadelphia, Pa.
W. F. Hall Printing Co., Chicago, Ill.
J. B. Lippincott Co., Philadelphia, Pa.
McCalla & Co. Inc., Philadelphia, Pa.
The Patteson Press, New York, New York
The Plimpton Press, Norwood, Mass.
Poole Bros., Chicago, Ill.
Edward Stern & Co., Philadelphia, Pa.
The Stone Printing & Mfg. Co., Roanoke, Va.
C. D. Traphagen, Lincoln, Neb.
The University Press, Cambridge, Mass.

For Composition

Boston Typothetae School of Printing, Boston, Mass.
William F. Fell Co., Philadelphia, Pa.
The Kalkhoff Company, New York, N. Y.
Oxford-Print, Boston, Mass.
Toby Rubovits, Chicago, Ill.

For Electrotypes

Blomgren Brothers Co., Chicago, Ill.
Flower Steel Electrotyping Co., New York, N. Y.
C. J. Peters & Son Co., Boston, Mass.
Royal Electrotype Co., Philadelphia, Pa.

H. C. Whitcomb & Co., Boston, Mass.

For Engravings

American Type Founders Co., Boston, Mass.
C. B. Cottrell & Sons Co., Westerly, R. I.
Golding Manufacturing Co., Franklin, Mass.
Harvard University, Cambridge, Mass.
Inland Printer Co., Chicago, Ill.
Lanston Monotype Machine Company, Philadelphia, Pa.
Mergenthaler Linotype Company, New York, N. Y.
Geo. H. Morrill Co., Norwood, Mass.
Oswald Publishing Co., New York, N. Y.
The Printing Art, Cambridge, Mass.
B. D. Rising Paper Company, Housatonic, Mass.
The Vandercook Press, Chicago, Ill.

For Book Paper

American Writing Paper Co., Holyoke, Mass.
West Virginia Pulp & Paper Co., Mechanicville, N. Y.